EMPOWERING THOUGHTS

Written by
JAMES COLE

Edited by
Alex Knysh

Empowering Meditations
10 Birtinya Court
Frankston, 3199
Australia

© 2019 by James Cole

All rights reserved. No part of this book may be reproduced in any form or by any means, electronic or mechanical, including photocopying, recording, or by any information storage and retrieval system, without permission in writing from the copyright holder.

Published by Empowering Meditations
EmpoweringMeditations.com

EMPOWERING THOUGHTS

Thank you to:

My parents Alan and Janet Cole for all they have given me.

Alex Knysh for your constant support, encouragement, help and friendship.

Brad Armel for your friendship and always pushing me to see other perspectives.

Kyla De Graauw for showing me a new path.

Catherine Bell for sharing your magic.

Glen Murdoch for seeing my worth when I could not.

Mr. John Collins for introducing me to meditation. The black cat lives on.

And everyone who has been part of my journey.

You are all loved
James Cole

For Sarah McShane

Without you, this would not exist.

How to use this book

Although you can start at the start and read to the end, this is not the intended way for reading this book. Beyond the prologue, it is not intended to be linear. Think of it as sparks of ideas, bursts of passion, nuggets of wisdom, and thoughts to present different perspectives than your own.

Focus on whatever you are going through, or maybe, to simply set a line of thought or intention for the day. Then flick to a random page and read the message your unconscious mind has guided you to.

Meditate on it and how it relates. Seek a greater understanding of yourself with the thought you are presented with. And maybe, just maybe, you will have an amazing and life-changing moment of inspiration.

Introduction

My life was falling apart. I was thirty-nine years old and my twenty-year career had ended, and my relationship at the time was about to follow suit. My health was failing, and my body felt like it was falling apart. I say that, although I should really state that it was I who was failing my health.

My world was filled with conflict at every turn. People chasing me for the payments I missed, banks taking money from my accounts to pay credit debt leaving nothing for rent or anything else, corporate sociopaths trying to manipulate me into working for them for nothing, and on and on it went.

I remember the moment clear as day. I stood alone in my studio, surrounded by memorabilia of a broken life. My adrenal gland in its permanently heightened state of relentless stress and anxiety. Normally I would retreat. Shut it all out. Cower to my inner darkness. Block out the light, turn up some dark heavy music and surrender to the deep depression that felt so familiar and safe.

But this day was different. Gone was the usual self-punishing questions of WHY's; Why me? Why is everything falling apart? Why am I so shit?

No, this day was different. From my lips pushed a new type of question. One I was unaccustomed to. As the phone lowered from my ear at the end of a particularly intense argument with a bank manager, the question escaped.

"How can I get rid of these arseholes?"

It wasn't polished but what is when in a state of despair.

I didn't realise it at the time, but the simple act of changing my usual 'why' question to a 'how' question, set in motion a ripple through my reality that would change everything.

Defeated and deflated, I raised the phone once again, this time to check on Facebook. Maybe someone somewhere liked one of my posts and therefore liked some part of me. Gratification in its most pathetic form. It seemed fitting.

As the screen loaded, before me was an image with text over it. A meme as they have come to be known. I'd seen thousands before. But this one was different. As I read the words, it was as if they shone a beam of light directly into my soul. I knew... I just knew this was the answer to my 'how' question moments before. It simply read

"Stop complaining for 24 hours and see what difference it makes."

What did I have to lose, right? I was scraping the bottom of the proverbial rock. In my deepest confusion, this Facebook meme shone a light on the exit sign. I still had to put the effort into reaching that exit myself, but at least I had a direction.

"I can do that," I thought "how hard could it be?"

Over the next twenty-four hours, I gained greater self-awareness than the previous thirty-eight years combined. I came to realise just how much complaining I was actually doing.

There was the usual venting to friends and family but then there was all the conflict going on in my head. I would complain to myself constantly. Thinking about all the things I'd done wrong or the wrongs that others had done to me. Playing them over and over with guided commentary of how useless I was, how cowardly I was, how pathetic and worthless I was. I would even feel myself flush; furiously burning in my cheeks and chest as I relived my most distressing moments.

And what's worse, if I couldn't think of anything to complain about at that particular moment, I'd create scenarios that if something happened on the last Friday in March when the Sun was setting and the planets aligned just wrong, then this 'thing' would happen and god damn I'm gonna bitch and moan about it and all the ways I could screw that up too.

My mind was a cesspit of poisonous thought patterns and I was amazed how it had escaped my awareness until I read a silly Facebook meme. What kind of loser was I?

And then I stopped.

I was doing it again. I was actually complaining about the thing that made me realise how much I complained about EVERYTHING.

At that moment, I burst out laughing. Laughing at the absurdity of it. What else could I do? It was so ridiculous. I was ridiculous. Everything was ridiculous.

As I laughed, I could feel the most negative and destructive energies within me dissipating. It all seemed so silly.

Eventually, the laughter subsided and I

became aware of more complaints entering my mind. I laughed again, and again the energies subsided.

"I can use this" I remember thinking.

From that day on, as soon as I became aware of complaining in my head, I started to laugh, forcing it if I had to. It didn't matter. The mere act of laughing, dissipated the negative energies every time.

Those twenty-four hours turned into days, then weeks, then months. Slowly but surely, my mind was being retrained. I was becoming aware of the complaints almost the moment they were being formed then shutting them down just as quickly.

Friends and family were commenting on how positive I seemed to be getting. And I was. Laughter had become my anti-venom and it was powerful.

Little by little, my life started to get back on track. Not only that, I was attracting a better type of people around me. New friends were replacing old ones that had once unknowingly reinforced my self-destructive ways.

Months turned into years and my health was returning too.

I had always been an exceptional learner, now my line of study was in personal development and living healthy. I soaked up everything I could that would help me to live better, to be better.

Then one day at an appointment with my psychologist at the time, Kyla, she asked me toward the end of an impassioned rant, "What do you want to do?"

It stopped me dead. I didn't know. I'd always known what I wanted to do in the past. Ever since a family trip to Universal Studios at six years of age, all I'd wanted was to make movies. And that's exactly what I'd spent the last twenty years doing.

And now, on the other side of this broken

dream, I didn't know what I wanted any more. I recalled the times I'd made fun of those 'losers' who were mid-life and still didn't know what they wanted to do. And yet here I was, now one of them.

To save face, I blurted out "I want to help people... I want to do what you do... Just without the nine years of university or whatever."

It was a throw-away comment, although, with some truth to it. I did want to help people. My life in the film industry had felt so self-indulgent. It was as if every aspect floated so delicately around the inflated egos of all involved. All the time taking and never giving. It had made my soul weary to be around such people of which I had also been one. Now I wanted nothing more than to give back to my fellow humans. To pay my karmic debt and live with peace in my heart.

Of course, I would never go back to school again. Traumatic memories of school days still haunted me on a daily basis. Being bullied in the yard, humiliated on the sports ground and generally a below-average student.

"If only he would apply himself instead of staring out the window." Was written on more report cards than I can remember. If only they understood, being in my own mind while gazing out of those windows was giving me a greater education than their rigidly structured, one size fits all, approach to teaching.

That night at home, I received an email from Kyla. She had made a list of all the different types of therapies that didn't require half a life at university. Intrigued, I read everything and visited every web site she had linked to. I took it all in. But one above all stood out to me. Life coaching.

I'd never even heard of 'life coaching' before this moment. Even the likes of legendary life coach Tony Robbins was but the faintest blip on my radar.

The next day I researched all I could find

about this intriguing vocation and the places to learn this curious endeavour. I called around and found that many of the colleges had a really pushy, scammy vibe to them. Something I was succinctly aware of from a brushing with a network marketing company in my early twenties.

My boss at the time introduced me to his "other business" and had taken me along to some meetings after work. I couldn't quite pinpoint what was wrong with the whole scenario, but I felt something was off.

Only later when I researched brainwashing techniques did I figure it out. Sleep deprivation by holding these meetings that would run til two or three in the morning on a work night, introducing alcohol with dinner, then high pressure ganging up on people and pounding their emotional triggers to breaking point, followed, of course, by offering a guiding hand, a way out of the chaos and confusion if you followed their plan. I'd seen it work on person after person but to this day have no idea why it didn't work on me.

The next day I called The Life Coaching College. Unlike many of the other colleges, they happened to be based only twenty minutes from my home. I spoke with the owner Glen and he invited me to visit for a chat. An hour or so later I was sitting in the school having visions of my future flashing before my eyes. I walked out with all the study materials, having no idea what I was doing or how I would pay for it. I knew only that I HAD to do it, as if some powerful force was guiding me down this path no matter what.

I recall sitting in that first class a week later, terrified, confused, surrounded by people I didn't know, talking about things I didn't understand, who all seemed better than me. An introvert's nightmare.

I pushed through and by the end of this first intensive week, I thought I knew a thing or two about NLP (neuro-linguistic programming). I was blown away by the ways the mind worked and could be affected. A subject that had always fascinated me.

Two years later and I really knew what NLP was all about, along with advanced coaching practices, Matrix therapies, hypnosis and a bunch of other skills and modalities.

Over this journey, each of us in the class must have received a decade's worth of therapy as we practised on each other again and again. As a result, I left the school unrecognisable to the person I had been when I entered. Yet it was only the beginning of this new journey.

The rage I'd carried deep inside for as long as I could remember, was gone. Along with it, the deep shame and sadness I'd always felt. At the age of forty-one, I finally felt like an adult emotionally.

Fascinated, inspired and my passion re-ignited, I delved deeper into subjects of the mind and how we as humans worked. Always experimenting and using all I learned on myself.

If there is such a thing as being born with a gift, mine is the ability to see the patterns and the mechanisms of how things work at a fundamental level. Once I understand the principles, I no longer require the details. My depth of understanding skyrocketed.

Along the way, I started to see clients; first as a life coach, then a hypnotist and finally as a meditation educator. Constantly reassessing and adapting to all forms of feedback.

Friends would reach out for help with all their problems and to gain a greater understanding and I was happy to share. The clients I attracted were often intrigued by the deeper questions of reality, even if they didn't pertain to their current issues. It's like they instinctively knew I'd be able to help them in some way. And help them I did.

As I would answer them, it's as if the words would flow from me without thought. I started catching myself as I was delivering these nuggets of wisdom and thinking "gee that's actually pretty good" and often it was something that I needed to hear too.

So, I began writing them down and as pages of notes started to mount up, I began to remember. I remembered my late teens and early twenties when I was first experimenting with meditation, consciousness and pushing my cognitive limits. A time before I entered the analytical world of filmmaking. A time when my creativity flowed freely, and I just wrote endlessly. Poetry, stories, thoughts, ideas, concepts, questions. My mind was tapped into something beyond myself.

I visited my parents' house and unpacked old boxes of notepads that had been sealed up decades before. As I read, it was as if I was witnessing the birth of my personality. There was so much depth to the words. A depth I didn't even begin to understand at the time. So many concepts and theories that had clearly been ticking over in the back of my mind for twenty years or more. And now I understood everything on a much deeper level. Ideas I had shared with clients and friends, were right there in their infancy. Some dating as far back as primary school.

And then it all came flooding back. A memory that had been buried deep within my unconscious mind. It felt so real, yet couldn't possibly be anything other than a dream. Could it?

A beach, waves, a symbol and a voice. Oh, that voice and the message that followed. An idea, an understanding of how it worked. How it *all* worked. I had just been a teenager at the time.

It's as if I needed to bury what happened in order to go out and experience life. To follow dreams, to have them crushed, to be metaphorically kicked and beaten, to love and to lose. I needed it all to understand the message that was given. And now, at forty-four years of age, was the time of understanding.

I gathered my notes from the past and the new ones from interactions with clients and read through them all. I needed to get this message out to others. Not to dictate how the Universe works and pretend that I have all the answers. That would, in fact, be against the very core of the message itself. No, the reason was simple. To give people a different perspective. To maybe wake them up to the possibilities of living an empowered life.

I don't claim to be perfect. I don't claim to even live the perfectly empowered life. All I know is that living by the words, thoughts and philosophies within my writings, I have climbed out from a pretty dark pit. One that almost saw me step off this planet on more than one occasion.

I know one thing for sure, the more I adopt these principles into my own life, the better everything becomes.

The thoughts in this book have changed my life in ways I couldn't have ever imagined, and they have the potential to change anyone who adopts them.

What will you do with the thoughts that follow?

Prologue

The child woke to the sounds of the ocean, waves crashing on the shore where sleep had been. Slowly, consciousness began to clear. The dream that was, now dispersing, making way for the vision that is the day.

One by one awareness of the other senses; the fresh smell of the ocean breeze, salty taste in the air, scratchy feel of the sand beneath and finally eyes opening to the spectacle of the world around.

Only, something was askew. Superimposed upon the vista, a symbol. Hanging in the air, burning with furious passion of the purest light. Wherever the child turned, there it was. A swirl, a stroke and three more. A hallucination, a remnant from another place. Blindingly bright yet soothing and calm. A light of peace, a symbol of power.

And then came the voice. At first as if behind, then realisation that the voice was from within.

"Who are you?" asked the child.

"I am Tashuk-Rei, the empowered master." The voice responded with absolute authority.

"Where are you?"

"I am" the master's voice paused for a moment. "Somewhere else"

"What is this symbol I see before me?"

"This is your symbol. A symbol of power. It burns for you. A light in the darkness of confusion and chaos. A light to guide you. A light to remind you of that which you are."

"I am but a small child" he responded.

"Yes, this is true." A moment passed in contemplation "And so much more."

"I do not understand master."

"I know. This is why I am here. To teach you. To guide your thoughts so you can understand and live with a true sense of power."

EMPOWERING THOUGHTS

The child stood motionless, transfixed on the symbol and mesmerised by the master's voice.

"Are you ready to learn?" Asked the master.

The child nodded agreement and the symbol transformed into the figure of Tashuk-Rei, the empowered master.

"Let us begin" the master stated.

And the journey of empowerment commenced.

EMPOWERING THOUGHTS

EMPOWERING THOUGHTS

There is breath in the space between heaven and sea, between sea and land, between land and the heavens.

An eternal pause, a forever moment.

A magical place where all is possible, where dreams and reality are one.

Stop!

Breathe it in.

Reconnect with what you are.

Become one with the eternal.

For what you will find there is love.

And what you will know is you.

The empowered person understands that no matter how convincing personal perception is of being an absolute truth, it is actually only one of an infinite truths.

Silence is the place where magic happens.

EMPOWERING THOUGHTS

The empowered person knows that seeking change in others, will only find conflict, while seeking change in self, will find only lessons.

Stressed?

Breathe slow

Breathe deep

Be still

The empowered person knows that in letting go of the emotion, all that remains is the lesson.

While everyone else is seeking equality, the empowered person knows that only in embracing diversity will it bring us the complete human experience.

EMPOWERING THOUGHTS

The empowered person knows the more they own the more they are owned.

And the child asked, "Master, why is the world this way?"

And the master replied "The world isn't what you think it is...

It's what you *think* it is!"

EMPOWERING THOUGHTS

The empowered person is aware of anything that tries to externalise their power. They know that true power comes from within and to externalise is to give that power away.

The greatest power is in letting go.

The empowered person understands that everything they are is made up of the stories they tell themselves. Stories of their past, present and future. Clouded by a lifetime of emotions and limited perceptions.
To change who they are, how they act, and what they'll become, they know they must first change the stories they tell themselves.

Sometimes all that is needed for the pain to disappear is for another to understand our pain.

EMPOWERING THOUGHTS

The empowered person knows that giving up responsibility is the same as giving up their personal power.

By stepping into their confidence, the empowered person knows that their confidence will step into them.

The empowered person knows that a habit is just a thought they keep thinking. And by changing the thought, they change the habit.

Light is always light.

Light is never dark.

No matter how dim the light becomes, it is still light and light is always beautiful.

Even when so faint you must cup your hands around and look ever so closely to see, it is still light.

When you gaze into the embers, the dull glow deep in the burning wood is still light and mesmerising and beautiful.

Suddenly it falls, just a little and a million illuminating sparks dance up into the sky in a spectacular display, each and every one of them beautiful and born of the faintest light of the glowing embers.

Light is always light.

Light is always beautiful.

You are light.

The empowered person knows to ask themselves "how much time do I dedicate to that which is most important to me?" and then adjust accordingly.

Love never asks for anything or takes anything.

Real love is only given or received.

EMPOWERING THOUGHTS

The empowered person knows that if they want someone to be better, the way to teach them is by showing with their own actions.

EMPOWERING THOUGHTS

From knowledge comes empowerment!

EMPOWERING THOUGHTS

The empowered person knows they are here to have an earthly experience so they can expand the Universe to what it wasn't without them.

Appreciate your weakness
for it shows you your strength.

EMPOWERING THOUGHTS

The empowered person understands that by hiding from their darkness, they will never enlighten it.

One of the biggest mistakes we make is to think we are separate and external from nature when nature is really all there is.

The empowered person understands that 'logic' can be used to justify anything and can be their strongest armour and their greatest enemy.

EMPOWERING THOUGHTS

Self-worth heals many wounds.

EMPOWERING THOUGHTS

The empowered person prepares for the worst, hopes for the best, and expects nothing.

All too often love and possession are confused as the same thing. The empowered person recognises that real love is about freedom, not possession.

EMPOWERING THOUGHTS

The empowered person knows that by meditating they will discover answers to questions they never even knew they needed to know.

EMPOWERING THOUGHTS

You are good enough!

You are worthy!

End of story!

The empowered person knows that those who brag the least often have the most to brag about.

EMPOWERING THOUGHTS

When your world is filled with CHAOS,

Be Still,

Be Calm,

Be Strong.

That which is inner becomes that which is outer.

EMPOWERING THOUGHTS

The empowered person is never afraid of ending a relationship.

When a relationship no longer works, they know that by holding on, they dig in, making the scars deeper.

By separating, they give space for the relationship to either heal and evolve or create space for something new.

I spent my whole life building strength and fighting against everything, only to realise that real strength comes from letting go and not reacting in the first place.

Everyone wants to change the world, and yet so few are willing to change themselves. It is only in changing the self that their world will be changed.

The empowered person knows that as society strives to give up all individual responsibility, the path to empowerment is to take it all back.

We trust our senses implicitly.

Yet our senses are only there to trick us into believing we are something other than what we truly are!

The empowered person appreciates that everything is important until they realise it's not.

Carried on the winds of time, breath is the bond between the realms of consciousness and spirit.

The empowered person understands that every action has a consequence. As does every inaction.

"Master I cannot meditate, my mind is too busy."

"Of course child, your breath is hurried and shallow. As you slow your breath to the depths of your belly, consciousness will become focused and introspective.

Meditation will become inevitable."

EMPOWERING THOUGHTS

The empowered person recognises that however a person believes the Universe works, they are correct.

Never underestimate the power of imagination.

It is where all that is began.

The empowered person recognises that the reason any of us are anything is that we believe we are and act accordingly.

EMPOWERING THOUGHTS

"Master, why do people take so much medicine when they feel down?"

"Because child, they have not realised they have the power to meditate and heal within them. Instead, they would rather pay for external poisons in the guise of cures than converse with their inner world."

The empowered person acknowledges that everything is just an idea, discovered or created by a person with perceptions just as flawed as their own.

Ideas followed are chosen wisely.

Nothing is sadder than a person blindly following the dogma of religion.

Each of us was given a unique piece of the infinite puzzle that contributes to our greater understanding of the Universe as a whole.

Religion teaches to discard our own piece of that puzzle in order to follow somebody else's.

EMPOWERING THOUGHTS

The empowered person knows they are never too old for play.

EMPOWERING THOUGHTS

Just breathe.

The empowered person honours the past by learning from the achievements and mistakes of their history.

They can then build on that knowledge with the power of hindsight to achieve greater wisdom and understanding for today and a prediction of what may come tomorrow.

EMPOWERING THOUGHTS

Nothing matters except that which matters to you.

The empowered person understands that sometimes the best reaction is no reaction.

"Master I am but a small child, insignificant to the immense forests and endless oceans."

"Child, it is good to be humbled by nature.

Stare out into the ocean, gaze up at the heavens, get lost in a forest, wander the desert sands.

Feel the infinite scope of that which you are only a tiny part of.

Yet a part of it you are and without you, it would be incomplete."

The empowered person sees that the world around them is a reflection of their world within.

EMPOWERING THOUGHTS

Logic is whatever you want it to be.

The empowered person has reclaimed complete ownership of their state of mind, being, all that they do and all of the consequences of their actions.

They recognise that it is only in taking complete responsibility for themselves that they can live the empowered life.

When the empowered person feels stressed, they know to ask, "Would I be stressed if this happened a year ago, or five or ten and I only just found out?"

They see how their perception of time affects their perception of reality.

The empowered person recognises that good and evil are merely ideas of humankind.

In truth there only is or is not!

EMPOWERING THOUGHTS

Find the beauty in everything

pleasure in all you do,

and wisdom in all that is.

The empowered person knows to focus on what they want rather than what they do not.

We are all ONE!

This does not mean we are all one species, although we are.

This does not mean we are all connected, although we are.

This does not mean we are all a part of something bigger, although we are.

It means,
We are all ONE!

The empowered person knows that if love comes with conditions, it is not love.

EMPOWERING THOUGHTS

When you feel you have no time to stop, that is the time you need to stop.

We are all someone's idiot.

The empowered person remembers this when they are about to judge another.

EMPOWERING THOUGHTS

There's a pervasive myth that the way things are, is the way they should be.

The empowered person flows like the wind, embracing obstacles and change to enhance their own power and sculpt their reality.

Sometimes it's good to shake off the human and return to spirit for a while.

Meditate!

EMPOWERING THOUGHTS

The empowered person knows that expectations are the root of all disappointments.

"Master, I am here!"

"Are you sure child? Cause from here you are there."

The empowered person sees that we live in a Universe of infinite complexity and infinite simplicity and knows that where they focus is what they'll be.

Oh, how convoluted we make the simplicity of life.

The empowered person knows that confidence comes from the choice to act as if they are confident and the true confidence will follow.

"Master, I am so stupid and annoyed with myself."

"Child, be kind and gentle with yourself. You are the only self you have."

EMPOWERING THOUGHTS

The empowered person comprehends that boredom is doing nothing when not wanting to do nothing.

By changing that nothing into something, there is no longer boredom.

That something can be as simple as thinking, contemplating or meditating.

There is no reason to ever be bored in an infinite Universe.

People often confuse determination and stubbornness.

The empowered person knows that only determination will get them to their destination. Stubbornness will hold them exactly where they are.

EMPOWERING THOUGHTS

The empowered person feels that meditation is like having an intimate date with the most authentic version of themselves.

Nothing is forever.
Not even death.

EMPOWERING THOUGHTS

The empowered person understands that once they have learned all they can from a relationship, the bond is released.

By holding on beyond this time, the relationship will be become damaged, often beyond repair.

By letting go, they can drift apart intact, leaving room for their paths to cross again for future learnings.

"Master I do not have time to practice today, I will make time tomorrow."

"Child, you cannot 'make' time. Become aware of how much this concept of time influences your thoughts, your language, your beliefs and how you live your life, and you will realise that NOW is all you have. Only then will you understand just how destructive the illusion of time is."

The empowered person knows that to love another is to love oneself.

Without love of self, there can be no love for others.

EMPOWERING THOUGHTS

What is one thing you can forgive right now?

The empowered person sees angels and demons as the same, merely from different perspectives.

The veil of reality is so fragile. The empowered person understands that when they hold on so tightly to its projection, the slightest disruption that occurs, causes immense struggle in coping with the shift.

They know to let go of rigidity and accept that reality is fluid, constantly changing; ebbing and flowing with the currents of thought.

EMPOWERING THOUGHTS

The empowered person understands that the power of imagination is greater than any imagined power.

"Master, what of those people who sit around watching television, do nothing and contribute nothing, wasting their lives away?"

"Just because you do not see value in what they are doing, does not mean there is none. The Universal experience contribution of the couch potato is just as valuable as that of the pioneer."

EMPOWERING THOUGHTS

The empowered person recognises that one of their greatest strengths is to be compassionate toward themselves.

The sad truth is, once the magic is understood, no longer will the magic exist.

The good part is that there is more magic in the world than anyone could possibly know.

EMPOWERING THOUGHTS

The empowered person understands that everything exists, limited only by the filters of perception.

Within an infinite Universe, everything is.

EMPOWERING THOUGHTS

The empowered person understands there is NO time; NO past, NO future; and all exists as one, simultaneous present.

"Master, I am confused."

"Well child, think about that confusion.

Think about that thought you thought you'd thought but never did.

That just became a thought to think about did it not?

And as you think about that thought you thought, allow all thoughts to unravel from chaos into order now"

EMPOWERING THOUGHTS

The empowered person knows that if they want to feel powerful, all they have to do is stand and breathe as if you are powerful.

"Master, I am so desperate to learn but I just don't understand"

"Child, the energy of desperation can be ugly and holds the frequency of repulsion rather than attraction. Let it go and what you seek will come."

The empowered person knows that it is never the heart they cannot trust. It is the voices they allow to be louder than the heart that are untrustworthy.

The list of things that one does not want is literally infinite.

The empowered person knows that by focusing on what they *do* want, they begin attracting that energy into their reality.

EMPOWERING THOUGHTS

The empowered person knows that to change their language is to change their reality.

"Remember child, everyone is an expert of something."

"Even those who do nothing?"

"Yes, for they are the experts of doing nothing as it is what they spend their time doing."

EMPOWERING THOUGHTS

The empowered person knows to STOP and ask, "Have I made time for ME today?"

Somewhere between nothing and everything, is you.

The empowered person understands that when their soul is running on empty, everything becomes more difficult.

Nourishing the soul is just as important as feeding the body.

When their soul is full, nothing can bring them down.

EMPOWERING THOUGHTS

Breathe in

Breathe out

Let go

Repeat

EMPOWERING THOUGHTS

The empowered person understands that when they are stressed all they seek is a way out, losing focus and rationality.

In these moments they STOP and BREATHE, slow and steady.

By allowing a moment to let go they create a mental state of clarity that enables them to take focused action towards their desired outcome.

"Master, how do I control my destiny?"

"Child, when you realise there is no control, only perception of realities, you achieve a freedom to move between them, to perceive and therefore exist in the reality of your choosing."

EMPOWERING THOUGHTS

The empowered person knows the opposite of stress is relaxation and the most effective way to relax is by meditating.

Only a fool would discard the words of religious teachings.

Only a fool would follow them blindly.

The empowered person knows that by focusing on the breath, they become aware of the autonomous systems of life.

When they consciously slow their breath, they are taking control of the autonomous and sculpting it to their will.

Recognising that reality is the autonomous nature of existence, they also understand that meditation is the key to sculpting reality into whatever they want it to be.

There is only now.

And now is everything.

EMPOWERING THOUGHTS

The empowered person knows to ask themselves "What's one thing I can do today to make my tomorrow better?"

"Master, I do not have time to meditate today."

"Child, that is the whole point. Meditating slows your perception of all that is, granting you even more of this illusion of time."

The empowered person knows to look at FEAR as a guiding light for what they must confront to live in complete FREEDOM

People feel safe in the comfort of illusion.

There is a truth behind the facade of reality that seldom seek.

EMPOWERING THOUGHTS

The empowered person recognises that the path to enlightenment is wrought with pain. As they evolve, they shed layers of hurt. Each layer becoming more painful as more of the wound is exposed. Until one day they shed the wound itself and forget how painful it ever was, being left with only the lessons learned and the memory of who they used to be.

The most unassuming faces have the deepest stories.

The empowered person understands that resisting change does not mean the change will not occur.

It means they will not find the enjoyment within it.

Change is constant. One moment to the next, nothing ever stays the same.

"Imagine a child; cold, lost, hurt, and beaten down by life. How would you treat this child?"

"Master, I would show the deepest compassion and help the child however I could."

"Treat your heart, mind and soul the same as if they were that child, for they have been through a lot."

The empowered person knows being busy is meaningless without accomplishments.

And accomplishments are meaningless without the reflection to appreciate them.

EMPOWERING THOUGHTS

As a new day begins

Breathe out your yesterday

Let go of all that it was

Breathe in your today

Become aware of the possibilities that await

Now that your past is closed and your future is open

Become one with the now

Breathe in

Breathe out

Just Be!

EMPOWERING THOUGHTS

The empowered person knows the more they feel the less they think.

"Child, you know the practice of decluttering where you hold on to something and if it brings you joy, keep it and if it doesn't, let it go?"

"I do master"

"Do that with your thoughts and emotions too."

The empowered person knows a habit is just something that was done repeatedly until the habit was acquired.

They understand that old habits can be changed and new ones acquired simply through different repetition.

It is a strange and wonderful web the Universe weaves.

The empowered person knows that every choice they make today affects not only themselves tomorrow, but every future generation to come.

"Master, I cannot meditate, there is too much noise"

"Child, when I sit down to meditate and the dog starts to bark and the children yell and scream as they play and the heavens rumble and the birds squawk, I pause, take a breath and think to myself, oh thank goodness I'm about to meditate and close my awareness to all that noise."

EMPOWERING THOUGHTS

The empowered person knows to let go of how they "should" be, focus on what they want to become, then act accordingly.

EMPOWERING THOUGHTS

Stop!

Just stop!

For a single moment.

Put everything down.

Your possessions, your schedules, your worries, your thoughts.

Put them all down and just stop.

Breathe.

Be still.

Be calm.

Breathe in peace and tranquillity.

Breathe out and let go

Just a moment.

Now continue your day.

The empowered person understands that the Universe is infinite and eternal which means all possibilities exist. Whatever they choose to believe, is the perception of the Universe that will open up to them and the Universe will provide all the evidence they need to reinforce this belief.

We only know a person for the pieces they share, yet what is hidden makes up the depth of their character.

EMPOWERING THOUGHTS

The empowered person understands that nothing matters except that which matters to them.

The empowered person recognises that everything they are is based on what they have been taught.

The lessons of today will form who they become tomorrow.

You can handle it, or you wouldn't be doing it. Your strength runs deeper and more powerful than you know.

The empowered person changes the world by changing themselves.

EMPOWERING THOUGHTS

"Master, with all these thoughts, my mind could never be still enough to meditate."

"Stop child. Close your eyes and breathe. Imagine yourself sitting here with me as you are. Become aware of all those thoughts within. Now imagine you are imagining yourself sitting here with me and watch yourself watching those thoughts. Allow the other you to experience those thoughts while you sit in stillness, quiet and calm."

The empowered person recognises that we can have knowledge without understanding it. Just as we can understand things without truly knowing them.

However you believe the Universe works, you are correct.

The empowered person knows that it is never a waste of time to indulge in their thoughts.

After all, thought is all we really have.

EMPOWERING THOUGHTS

What magical sights
this illusion conjures for us.

The empowered person knows that their outer world reflects their inner world. If there is conflict in their life, they know to reflect upon and release the conflict that lies within.

"Master, why must I clean, it is taking time away from my meditations?"

"Sometimes child, the best meditation can be to take something dirty and clean it, I mean really clean it, til it sparkles. Meditate on this while you clean."

The empowered person understands that their own self-love is the only love that matters when healing.

EMPOWERING THOUGHTS

You don't get anything if you don't ask for it and you'll be amazed at what you can get when you do.

The empowered person accepts that it is okay to not like some things. But it would be foolish to not like what they do not know.

Until we move past this idea of limitations, we'll be limited in everything we do, individually and as a species.

The empowered person recognises that sometimes they must walk away knowing all they have done is plant a seed. A seed that may take years to sprout and years more to reach harvest.

The empowered person lives in the present, knowing that what is done is done and what is to come is but a choice away.

Recognising that the present is all there really is, frees them from attachments of what was and will be.

Eventually, all emotions are dealt with.

Either on your terms or theirs.

EMPOWERING THOUGHTS

The empowered person understands that one of the most destructive forces in the world is a mind corrupted by an ego that believes its truth is the only truth.

May this day bless you with a kiss from an angel, a touch of magic, the spirit of joy and the light of a thousand stars.

EMPOWERING THOUGHTS

The empowered person affirms that today I am grateful for all the hurt and pain that has led me to joy and happiness.

The only approval required by the empowered person is that of their own heart.

The empowered person knows that compassion is like a muscle.

The more they exercise it, the stronger their compassion will become.

The debate over "free will OR fate" is an interesting bind we have put ourselves in. It could be that we have both, neither or something entirely different.

The empowered person is not granted the illusion of certainty. Certainty is for those who retreat into the safe facade of comfort and apathy.

EMPOWERING THOUGHTS

Change your language
Change your life!

The empowered person always allows time for others. They understand that others are merely themselves experiencing a different reality.

Allow the light of peace to burn so brightly within that it ignites the unburnt wick within those with no spark.

EMPOWERING THOUGHTS

The empowered person never states, "this is how it is done!" Instead, they ask "how can this be done better?"

When the sea is so tranquil. Not even the slightest sound of the tiniest ripple. Not too warm, not too cold, the air is fresh but still, as if the Earth herself is meditating.

Today I breathe as she breathes and accept her purity into my soul.

The empowered person recognises that connection with others can last a moment or a lifetime. They know the length of time has no determination over the depth of impact the connection may have on each other.

"Master I have so many questions."

"Child, All the answers to all the questions, lay deep in meditation. The deeper you listen the deeper the answers will be."

EMPOWERING THOUGHTS

The empowered person understands that today's peak is tomorrow's foothill.

Stop!

Look around you.

What do you see?

Find something beautiful about it.

Beauty is always there if you look deeply enough.

The empowered person understands that just because they always have, doesn't mean they always have to.

Only when every possible form of suffering has been experienced from every possible perspective will suffering become obsolete.

EMPOWERING THOUGHTS

The empowered person thinks to ask themselves what patterns can I let go of today that no longer serve me?

EMPOWERING THOUGHTS

We live in a web of assumptions.

The first is that reality is real.

EMPOWERING THOUGHTS

The empowered person understands that seeking ownership and possession is a sure way to enslave themselves.

EMPOWERING THOUGHTS

From the deepest confusion
grow the seeds of clarity.

EMPOWERING THOUGHTS

The empowered person understands that whenever they rely on technology to do something for them, they lose the ability to do it for themselves.

EMPOWERING THOUGHTS

Time is irrelevant!

EMPOWERING THOUGHTS

The empowered person knows that the world is what they choose to see.

EMPOWERING THOUGHTS

While you think those thoughts you cannot not think,

Stop,

Pull back.

Observe yourself think that you are thinking them.

Notice them drift into your mind and float away.

Into your mind and far away.

And now the knot is untied to those thoughts you did think,

Reenter your mind where the thoughts are no more.

The empowered person knows that the beauty of thoughts is that they can be changed.

Life feeds on life. This is the undeniable truth of existence. Everything living sources its energy from something else that is living. And eventually, everything living becomes food for some other life.

EMPOWERING THOUGHTS

The empowered person knows to defend their time fiercely.

EMPOWERING THOUGHTS

The size of the ripple depends entirely on how close the perspective.

EMPOWERING THOUGHTS

The empowered person is kind to all things, big, small, friend or foe.

When realisation occurs that we are all one, the only prejudice that can be held, is against oneself.

EMPOWERING THOUGHTS

The empowered person knows their actions echo out into the world and return even stronger.

"Each and every one of us contributes to the greater Universe in our own way"

The child ponders for a moment. "But what could I possibly contribute to the Universe master?"

"Experience child. Without you and your contribution to the well of all experience, the Universe is incomplete."

The empowered person knows that meditation can be as simple as relaxing their body and mind or as dramatic as changing their entire reality.

EMPOWERING THOUGHTS

Stop!

Breathe!

Focus on one point.

Expand your awareness.

Let it grow.

What do you see all around you?

What do you hear all around you?

What do you feel all around you?

Come back.

Continue.

The empowered person understands the reason we all have different experiences is so we don't have to fit all experiences into one life.

EMPOWERING THOUGHTS

Time is an illusion
designed to keep you small.

The empowered person knows that the surface is just for show and the truth lays deep within.

EMPOWERING THOUGHTS

All love matters.

The empowered person comprehends that free will is just an illusion as all possibilities already exist filtered by the limitations of perception. Change the perception and reality itself will appear to change.

The empowered person knows when they change their "why's?" into "how's?" their life will improve dramatically.

EMPOWERING THOUGHTS

If gratitude were currency... Be rich.

The empowered person knows to dedicate the majority of their energy toward that which is most important to their life.

"Master, I have heard people ponder questions like 'if we are all reincarnated, how are there so many more souls now than there have ever been?' Where do they all come from?"

"Child, there are no more souls than there ever were and no more than there ever will be. We are all but one soul having many experiences."

The empowered person understands that being able to receive is just as important as being able to give.

EMPOWERING THOUGHTS

Stop!

Remember who you are...

The YOU before the world buried you.

The YOU before you hid away.

Remember who YOU are.

Remember you are beautiful.

Remember you are perfection!

The empowered person understands that to put oneself first isn't just okay, it is necessary.

EMPOWERING THOUGHTS

The more distractions you allow, the more distracted you'll become.

The same works for focused attention.

The empowered person knows that by cutting distractions, focus will increase.

The empowered person accepts that everything anyone does, at its heart, is for selfish reasons... And that's okay.

"Master I have studied for many hours. I strive to be better."

"Child, in your pursuit to be better, remember to enjoy the now."

The empowered person understands that what they consume today is how they will feel tomorrow.

EMPOWERING THOUGHTS

You are the only one responsible for you.

The empowered person recognises that nobody *makes* them:

Say anything

Do anything

Feel anything

What they say, do and feel is always their own choice.

EMPOWERING THOUGHTS

Sleep is the medicine
that soothes all wounds.

The empowered person looks at everything as an opportunity to grow within.

There are too many wishy-washy, watered-down views in the world.

Ignite the passion within, own your truth and share it unapologetically with all who will listen.

The empowered person understands that total honesty with oneself is essential for an empowered life.

Once you accept that this is a ridiculous world, filled with ridiculous people, with ridiculous ideas and ridiculous beliefs, then you can let go of all that you take so seriously and have fun with sculpting your own level of ridiculousness.

The empowered person asks themselves the question "on a scale of 1 to 10, how much joy is in my life?"

Anything short of a perfect 10 is met with a second question "What can I do right now to raise that by one?"

"Master, I have some good ideas but I'm scared to share them in case they are stolen."

"Child, ideas are not yours to own. Ideas come from the divine portal that links your perception to the infinite. They are all that ever is, busting forth at just the right moment. Be assured, if you tune in to an idea, others will too. It is the first to share who receives the recognition, not the one who holds on from fear."

The empowered person understands they cannot reach the top of the ladder by skipping the bottom rungs.

We are all connected?

No.

We are one?

No.

I am all one!

Yes.

The empowered person knows that once they know the destination they seek, to ask themselves how it is they want to get there. The paths to any destination are infinite.

EMPOWERING THOUGHTS

Anxiety can strike even the empowered person. The difference is in the reaction. The empowered person follows four simple steps to release.

Stop

Breathe slow

Breathe deep

Be still

EMPOWERING THOUGHTS

The empowered person knows that the only truth worth living by is their own.

For everything else, they enjoy the story.

EMPOWERING THOUGHTS

We take life so seriously, often forgetting it's all just a game.

STOP

BREATHE

Find the fun. Find the beauty.

Play, create, laugh.

It's all there in all things, hiding just outside of serious.

EMPOWERING THOUGHTS

The empowered person understands that what they consume directly affects the quality of their thoughts.

Poison in, poison out.

Reality is merely a single path of perception for the infinite within.

Choose a different path, and reality will change.

The empowered person understands that there is no such thing as zero judgment, it's what they do in the moments after they've judged that matter.

Remember, those you judge are yourself having a different experience so that you don't have to.

EMPOWERING THOUGHTS

The empowered person recognises that their soul is unconditionally free and it's only their own thoughts that can enslave them.

EMPOWERING THOUGHTS

Learn the lesson

Let go of the emotion

Break the cycle

EMPOWERING THOUGHTS

The empowered person understands that enlightenment and happiness are not the same things. Happiness is only one emotion whereas enlightenment crosses all the emotions that are part of the human experience.

Life is too short...

If you consider eternity short.

The empowered person knows that what they focus on becomes their reality.

The illusion of time is so persuasive, it has us doing all manner of crazy things, distracting us from our truth.

EMPOWERING THOUGHTS

The empowered person knows that life is just a game and if they were to resist the game, they would be resisting the joy and fun in life.

We spend so much time holding back our true thoughts, feelings and desires because of fear...

The empowered person may still feel the fear yet pushes through and speaks their truth.

The empowered person knows that the future and the past are merely figments of imagination.

Neither one having power over them.

With each new learning, the empowered person knows they are only one small step of an infinite journey closer to understanding the Universe.

The empowered person understands that we each have our own interpretation of what reality is.

It is in piecing these interpretations together that we get to experience the whole.

When we ascend beyond the illusion of time, we realise we are all things.

EMPOWERING THOUGHTS

The empowered person understands that the mind interprets every bit of input it receives from their senses, based on what it already knows and understands.

With this understanding they know to take all input questioningly.

Gathering, not dismissing, different perspectives is what helps the empowered person to grow and evolve.

EMPOWERING THOUGHTS

The empowered person knows that every thought and every belief they have is based on an idea created by a human trying to make sense of the infinite Universe, just the same as they are.

They hold on to these thoughts and beliefs loosely, and only for as long as they serve them.

Let go of the illusion of time and all things are not only possible, they already exist.

EMPOWERING THOUGHTS

The empowered person knows that the perfect time to meditate is whenever they can.

"Master, what of those who claim they can speak with the dead?"

"Child, no-one can speak with the dead. They are dead! The question to ask instead is can we converse with those who exist outside our perception of time in the eternal now?

And the answer is yes!"

The empowered person knows to be grateful for those they despise the most, as they are the ones expressing certain realities so that they don't have to.

The empowered person understands that everything they have done in the past and everything they are doing in the present is helping to create their future. They understand that the burden of responsibility is theirs alone.

EMPOWERING THOUGHTS

There is nothing more beautiful than the magical spells of words, language, and communication.

The ability to take thoughts, visions, or feelings and convert them into the sounds that make up language. These sounds then vibrate their frequencies through the air to oscillate the ear of another, who then decodes this into sound which is translated back into thoughts, visions and feelings creating synaesthesia between the senses.

The empowered person understands that every experience is worthy for the one experiencing it. No matter how menial it may seem to others.

A moment in the moment has no meaning, it simply is.

Meaning comes from analysis once the moment has passed.

EMPOWERING THOUGHTS

The empowered person asks what will I do today to become more positive?

EMPOWERING THOUGHTS

The greatest source of conflict is one person believing their way is the only way.

The empowered person knows that comfort feeds apathy and apathy is the enemy of growth.

EMPOWERING THOUGHTS

We must be careful of the words we use.

They are the designs for the reality of tomorrow.

The empowered person knows that it is only in the self-awareness of recognising their own flaws that they are able to grow beyond them.

When something offends the empowered person, they use it as a guide to grow within rather than demand the outer world change to suit them.

The empowered person always asks, what can I do today to bring greater meaning to my existence?

EMPOWERING THOUGHTS

Honour the past

Live in the present

Create the future

Love eternal

The empowered person recognises that love is the raw energy from which the Universe is built.

All forms of creation are an expression of love.

All emotions are an expression of love.

Love is eternal and it is our individual expressions of love that create our reality.

EMPOWERING THOUGHTS

I leave behind all that I was.
Gather around me all that I am.
Create all that I will be.

Letting go of all but the lessons learned.
Shining my light to guide those in darkness.

I will do better than I did before.
I will be better than I was before.

And in the everlasting now,
I remain present with pure heart
and relentless determination.

For it is nothing short of my own reality
I manifest now!

Epilogue

"Oh empowered master, with all you have taught and all I have learned, I still do not understand how my life can have significance, how I can be enough, when the Universe is so infinite and I am so small, nothing but a speck in the eternal cosmos?"

"Child, do you not see? You are the seas, you are the wind, you are the birds in the sky and creatures on the ground, you are a mere pebble in the stream and the mountain from which it flows, you are the heavens and the earth, you are all that is, all that was and all that ever will be. You are me and I am you.

And I, my child, I am the Universe!"

EMPOWERING THOUGHTS

About the Author

James Cole was born in England and moved to Australia with his parents at age thirteen. After an award-winning, twenty-year career as a film editor and visual effects artist, he walked away to follow a passion to help people empower their lives.

He now lives in the beach town of Frankston in Victoria, Australia, where he produces content for his website, teaching people how to meditate and live an empowered life, as well as running live workshops.

This is his first published book.

Learn more about James, meditation and empowering your life with the programs and workshops he runs, by visiting his website:

EMPOWERINGMEDITATIONS.COM

The Empowered Life Program

Learning to meditate is only the first step to living an Empowered Life. This powerful online program developed by James Cole will help you identify all the ways your power is being given away. Through personal habits, thoughts and choices to those around us affecting us negatively and those who are outright manipulating us for their own cause.

It will then introduce you to powerful guided meditations and techniques to let go of negative emotions, connections and attachments. You will learn the secrets to doing this yourself and turn them into healthy mental habits.

Create and then become the Empowered being you were destined to be, living with freedom and purpose, creating the life YOU want, not the one that others want for you. Stand in your own power and own it.

To learn more visit

EMPOWERINGMEDITATIONS.COM/EL

www.ingramcontent.com/pod-product-compliance
Lightning Source LLC
Chambersburg PA
CBHW031410290426
44110CB00011B/328